THE BEST
OF EDNA JAQUES

To: Bela.
Love from
Pierre Hargreaves
Xmas, 1979.
boo boo

WESTERN PRODUCER BOOK SERVICE

SASKATOON

1974

first printing 1966

second printing 1967

second edition 1974

WESTERN PRODUCER BOOK SERVICE

Saskatoon, Saskatchewan

Printed and Bound in Canada by MODERN PRESS

Poems selected from the following twelve books of poetry:

Drifting Soil	Roses in December
Wide Horizons	Britons Awake
Kitchen Window	Backdoor Neighbors
Dreams in Your Heart	Hills of Home
Beside Still Waters	Fireside Poems
Aunt Hattie's Place	Golden Road

Plus fifteen new poems never before published.

DEDICATED TO THE PIONEERS

To those brave valiant hearts who came west when it was little more than a wilderness.

I proudly claim to be one of them. My father homesteaded in 1902 near where the Briercrest village now is, and turned the first furrow between the Soo Line and the Dirt Hills. As a small child I walked in that first crooked furrow, half a mile long.

POEMS

WHEN I LOOK BACK

When I look back across the years it seems to me that as well as my path being paved with good intentions (there were quite a few of them too), my path was paved by good friends.

It started when I was fourteen and just beginning to write my bits of verse. Thomas Miller of *The Moose Jaw Times* was the first one, as far as I can recall, who laid a stepping stone of encouragement and made the path a little smoother for my timid feet.

We lived on a homestead near where Briercrest now is, it was thirty-five "prairie trail" miles from Moose Jaw, and it was my turn to go to town. So my brother Clyde and I started out at dawn one summer morning, in a lumber wagon with a quiet team of plow horses for the day-long trip. He being seventeen was considered a man. How lovely the prairie looked with dew still on the grass and meadow larks singing from every brier patch.

This trip was the BEGINNING for me. I had taken a couple of poems (written on the middle pages of a five-cent scribbler) and handed them to Mr. Miller. If he had been a dragon rising from the carpet I couldn't have been more afraid. But he read the poems, then spoke kindly to me and told me to keep on writing, just keep on.

After I left (I was told years later) he called a cub reporter in and pointed to my brother and I going up the street and said "that little girl will write her name across Canada some day." Fred Workman (who later became editor of the paper) nodded, and from that day, he too, became my kindly helper and gave me untold encouragement, just by being kind to me when I went in.

From here the path widened, and the white paving stones became more frequent. John Kerr of the old *Moose*

Jaw Herald would look at me and mutter "you never know where it comes from" and give me a couple of dollars to pave the way a bit.

My mother had always called me her "clever girl" and was proud of me (like all mothers are). A pat of her hand and a good Irish smile would cheer me up for days.

Napier Moore wrote: "If you are the Edna Jaques whose poems are appearing in *The Saskatchewan Farmer, Maclean's Magazine* would appreciate it if you would send us some from time to time." They used the odd one for years.

And for nearly twenty-five years *The Saskatchewan Farmer* printed them and gave me $1.50 each. They used one in nearly every issue until the paper went out of business.

John Wodell of *The Calgary Herald* encouraged me by buying my poems for over ten years. He used to call me into the office and talk a blue streak to me, warning me "never to stop writing."

Bernard McEvoy of *The Vancouver Province* (who looked like Santa Claus) was generous with his praise and support. I wrote poems for the *Province* for about seventeen years, until he retired and when the new editor came on, he thought all poets were crazy and I never sold another one to them.

Frank Williams of the *Winnipeg Free Press* not only bought my poems for years but kept me at it, during my second siege of homesteading when I was pretty discouraged. He would write and tell me to keep on, just keep on, telling me I "had something" and must never stop trying.

Mr. Maitland of *The Toronto Star* used my poems for nearly twenty years on the editorial page and paved a new road for me in Ontario, until his retirement, when the axe fell again.

Bluff Donald Gordon, now president of the CNR said in the foreword of the book *Backdoor Neighbors*: "What Robert Burns is to Scotland Edna Jaques is to Canada" and Mackenzie King told me shyly "I've been your ardent fan for over twenty years."

Nellie McClung said: "You have the gift, Edna dear, to ring bells in the hearts of people."

Some of the poems have gone far afield. "Flanders Fields", used in pamphlet form raised over a million dollars in the U.S.A. It was also used at the ceremony of the Unknown Soldier in Arlington cemetery near Washington and is inscribed on a scroll inside the chapel there.

"Thankful for What?" was voted by American newspapers the poem of the year.

"Farm Homes" was cast in bronze on a plaque forty-five feet high at the World's Fair in San Francisco.

"Man with a Lantern" has been used in our Canadian school books and in some of the school readers of Scotland.

May all the poems found within this book revive old memories and bring a measure of joy to readers as much as the invitation to publish this book has brought to me.

Edna Jaques
Willowdale, Ontario

HOMESTEADERS

Pushing the frontiers further
    Back with relentless hands,
Blazing the trail with a plowshare
    Far in the hinterlands;
Holding fast to their birthright,
    Born to the realm of toil;
Bearded, grim and unconquered,
    Ragged kings of the soil.

Building their lonely cabins,
    Staking their homestead claim;
Beating the trail to Somewhere,
    Steady, fearless and game,
Bounded by sky and muskeg,
    Hedged by the vast unknown,
Earning their hundred and sixty,
    Winning their fight alone.

Theirs is the dream eternal,
    Hills that are rugged and green;
Lure of the far horizon,
    Prairies, wind-swept and clean,
Visioning towns in the making.
    Faith in the untried lands,
Holding the country's future,
    Safe in their calloused hands.

from "BESIDE STILL WATERS"

1

THE PIONEER

He loved new trails — and I remember one
    That straggled south, he made it in the spring,
Bringing out lumber for a tiny shack,
    And there it stood a little shiny thing,
How brave it looked against the lonely plain,
    Flinging defiance to the wind and rain.

How young he was — how proud of his new farm
    His plow caressed the furrows as it turned
The brown clean sod to sweeten in the sun,
    Sunflowers yellow as butter newly churned,
Starred the new land, like candles set to show
    The feet of eager settlers where to go.

And now the years have gone like wasted toil
    (So many better things we might have done.)
But still the land is dear and still the wheat,
    Waves like a golden banner in the sun,
(But he went out today with shining sails,
    To pioneer new worlds, and make new trails).

from "BESIDE STILL WATERS"

FARM KITCHEN AT NIGHT

The kettle sings a low contented tune,
    The dog snores in her sleep behind the stove,
There is a mingled odor in the air
    Of apple pie and cinnamon and clove,
The smell of yeast — for mother set the bread
    In the blue pan before she went to bed.

Beyond the pantry door I catch a glimpse
    Of shiny milk pans on a narrow shelf,
A row of plates — the old brown cookie crock;
    A brimming water pail all by itself,
A little bracket lamp beside the door,
    Makes a small halo on the kitchen floor.

An old grey cat is sleeping on a chair,
    Paws folded in below her snowy chest,
She looks the picture of contented peace,
    Like an old lady waiting for a guest,
Her eyes blink softly as if half awake,
    Pale green like water in a mountain lake.

The kitchen has a fragrance of its own,
    Of porridge simmering in a blue pot,
Of kindling wood drying beneath the stove,
    And red coals glowing beautiful and hot,
There is a sense of joy and comfort there,
    In the old stove and cushioned rocking chair.

A feel of home and peace and fireglow,
That lovely modern kitchens do not know.

from "GOLDEN ROAD"

3

TO A MAN WITH A LANTERN

He moves within a ragged patch of light
    Doing his chores about the stable way,
A blot of dancing yellow in the night,
    As back and forth he goes for sheaves and hay.

Whistling he moves about his humble chores
    The friendly stock, the stable warm and dim,
Long moving shadows play about the floors,
    The horses softly neigh for oats to him.

The cattle stand beside the stanchions bare
    Yielding their snowy milk, its fragrant heat
Rises like incense on the frosty air,
    The bedding straw is gold beneath their feet.

A kitten rubs its face against his arm
    Purring its friendly trust, the dog is close
Wagging his stubby tail in happy charm,
    His master's love the only heaven he knows.

Ah, could we find more gracious life than this,
    Full days of toil and lovely brooding night,
Good food and love and windows through the mist
    And homes within a yellow patch of light.

from "BESIDE STILL WATERS"

OLD RANCHER

He makes his lonely fire of buffalo chips,
    Beside the little stone-rimmed water hole,
Eases the saddle on his patient horse,
    Then tethers him upon a sunny knoll,
Brews his strong tea in a small blackened pot,
    Then sips it from the tin cup piping hot.

Far as the eye can reach the prairies lie
    Through leagues of golden air, unpeopled, vast,
Along the coulee rim the willows grow,
    In little scrawny clumps that softly cast
A flickering shadow on the tawny grass,
    The heavens burning like a roof of brass.

Old buffalo bones lie bleaching in the sun
    A bit of broken hoof, a crumpled horn,
A rutted path skirting the coulee rim,
    A buffalo wallow deep and crudely worn,
A little patch of gleaming alkali,
    Shimmering against the deep blue of the sky.

He slings his lariat with careless ease,
    Fastens it loosely to a saddle thong,
Takes up the reins, digs in his shiny spurs,
    Whistling a gay tune as he jogs along,
Sensing — far off — an eager happy band,
    Of settlers coming in to claim the land.

from "ROSES IN DECEMBER"

OLD-FASHIONED ROCKER

An old-fashioned rocker as nice as you please,
    With a cretonne seat and a frill,
And a pot of petunias with fluted skirts,
    There on the window sill,
A pair of old spectacles twisted and bent,
    Laid on an open book,
And a mother grey as an autumn night,
    Tucked in a sunny nook.

An old-fashioned rocker that squeaks when she rocks,
    By a window that looks on the street,
Where children go by on their way to a show,
    On a Saturday afternoon treat,
An apron with lace that she crocheted herself,
    A fichu and cameo pin,
A place for her Bible in reach of her hand,
    And a footstool all faded and thin.

In the old-fashioned rocker she sings as she rocks,
    And looks so contented and cute,
Songs that are old as the hills but I swear
    Their music is sweet as a flute,
She talks to herself (like a child at her play)
    And I wonder what visions she sees,
As she whispers and smiles in her small quiet way,
    With an afghan spread over her knees.

Just an old-fashioned mother as sweet as a rose
    And a face that is placid and kind,
For there's peace in her heart like a river in June,
    And a blessed contentment of mind,
And I hope when my journey is nearing its end,
    There's a house with a rose-bordered walk,
And a window with curtains that faces the sun,
    And a rocker that squeaks when I rock.

from "ROSES IN DECEMBER"

TO A SEED MERCHANT

Your catalogue arrived today,
 Thanks for the cover bright and gay,
And all the lovely host it brought,
 Delphiniums, forget-me-not,
Nasturtiums clustered to one side,
 And pale pink roses for a bride.

Although the winter wind is blowing
 Here in my room are flowers growing,
Petunias in their gay attire,
 And marigolds like sacred fire,
With Canterbury bells to ring
 Above the tender fields of spring.

Outside my window blizzards rage
 But here upon the glowing page
They smile like lovely guests — and, oh,
 I am so glad that flowers grow
In books . . . I have them twice you see,
 Next summer in the yard, and here tonight
Beside the fire with me.

from "KITCHEN WINDOW"

8

THE FARM

This is the part of the day I love,
 When the kids are safe in their beds,
The old dog snoring behind the stove,
 And a few stars overhead.

The old black stove with its shiny hearth,
 A lamp with a golden glow,
The kitchen warm as a summer eve,
 However the winds do blow.

The cattle are snug in their quiet stalls,
 Their bedding is clean and warm,
And I like to think of them sleeping there,
 Out of the wind and storm.

There's a peace that the wide world never knows,
 On a farm on a winter night,
When the valleys are steeped in a shiny mist,
 And the hills are clothed in white.

Give me a home with an old-fashioned look
 A plant on the window sill,
A rocking chair and a braided rug,
 And a church just beyond the hill.

THE DISCIPLES

*(Written for the fine men who work in the
churches of Canada)*

They do not look like fishermen,
    These modern men I see,
And yet I know they follow Him,
    Like those of Galilee.

They serve the wine of sacrament,
    And pass the blessed bread
Among the faithful followers,
    Like those the Saviour fed.

They do not work among the nets,
    Or wear a seaman's cloak,
Or reap the golden barley fields,
    But still they bear His yoke.

They dress in ordinary style,
    As modern as can be,
And yet I know they follow Him,
    Like those of Galilee.

THANKFUL FOR WHAT?

Not for the mighty world, oh Lord tonight,
    Nations and kingdoms in their fearful might;
Let me be glad the kettle gently sings,
    Let me be thankful . . . just for little things.

Thankful for simple food and supper spread,
    Thankful for shelter and a warm clean bed,
For little joyful feet that gladly run
    To welcome me when all my work is done.

Thankful for friends who share my joy and mirth,
    Glad for the warm, sweet fragrance of the earth,
For golden pools of sunlight on the floor,
    For peace that bends above my lowly door.

For little friendly days that slip away,
    With only meals and bed, and work and play,
A rocking chair and kindly firelight,
    For little things . . . let me be glad tonight.

from "KITCHEN WINDOW"

THE FAITHFUL FEW

(To church workers)

Wherever you go and whatever you do,
    Always you'll find them the faithful few
Who stick when the others are tired and gone,
    The little handful who carry on,
Drab and weary but grit to the core,
    Carrying His banner forever more.

Keeping the Sunday school from despair,
    Playing the organ and leading in prayer,
Finding the money for books and cards,
    Planting trees in the parsonage yards,
Helping the preacher through thick and thin,
    Doing their bit with a cheerful grin.

Always you'll find them at church affairs
    Bringing in water and extra chairs,
Giving a hand at the carving too,
    Just anything . . . they are glad to do,
Washing the dishes with tucked up sleeve,
    The first to come — and the last to leave.

Only a precious few at the best,
    But over the world from the East to the West,
They've carried His kingdom with faithful hands,
    Setting it up in a hundred lands,
Teaching His word to the uttermost part,
    Holding the glory safe in their heart.

For as long as we've churches and pews to fill,
    God will find servants to do His will —
Plain little commonplace working folk,
    Eager and ready to bear His yoke;
Ever His kingdom with work to do,
    Safe in the hands of the faithful few.

from "KITCHEN WINDOW"

I LOVE NEW THINGS

I love new things — a new dress or a hat,
    A little flower . . . a bow of this or that,
A saucy veil . . . a new pin bright as gold,
    (Clothes look so woebegone when they are old).

I love a pair of shoes with shiny toes,
    A tiny clasp . . . and little perky bows,
A swinging skirt a bit above the knees,
    Gay as a summer morning . . . if you please.

I love new things when spring is at the door,
    And golden shafts of sunlight seem to pour
Across the lawns and scarlet flower beds,
    Where Johnny-jump-ups slowly nod their heads.

I love the newness of an April day,
    Spring in the air . . . and summer on the way,
A quiet meadow where a nuthatch sings,
    Above the shining lustre of new things.

KEEPSAKES

So many keepsakes we gather up,
    A willow plate or a Dresden cup,
The colored strands of a teapot stand,
    A lacquered box from the Holy Land.

Perhaps a doll with a rosy face,
    In a satin gown and a frill of lace,
With little slippers and beaded bows,
    And a tiny hat with a faded rose.

A little boy in a tarnished frame,
    A small wee fellow without a name,
That was lost somehow in the family tree,
    But he looks like old Uncle John to me.

A baby shoe . . . and a woolen shawl,
    An old settee in the upstairs hall,
A mustache cup and a tarnished star,
    A candle bought at a church bazaar.

These are the things that we sometimes keep,
No one knows why . . . but they haunt our sleep.

THE GREAT GRANDFATHER

He has no place or part in this today,
    His very bones are dust, his heart is clay,
And yet we follow little paths he laid,
    Walk in and out through sturdy doors he made.

His hands have crumbled down to golden soil
    And yet we reap the harvests of his toil,
The trees he planted by the carriage shed,
    Blossom and bear their apples warm and red.

His tired feet have long since found their rest,
    And yet the part of home we love the best,
Are little fields he plowed and worked alone,
    The pasture that he cleared of stump and stone.

The well he dug and curbed with careful hand,
    Still yields its clear sweet water from the land,
Bubbling up from the deep springs of earth,
    Old as the ancient hills . . . yet new as birth.

He does not die . . . but somewhere in the sun
    Forever lives the good that he has done —
The furrowed field . . . the budding apple tree,
    Bearing its fruit for children yet to be.

from "KITCHEN WINDOW"

FLAT LAND

I love flat land; flat as a table top
>   Holding upon its breast a growing crop
Of oats or barley . . . wheat in serried rows,
>   A trailing buckwheat vine that often grows
Amid the wheat as if to give it grace
>   Like a print apron with a frill of lace.

Deep bottom land they call it, fields that hold
>   The heavy strength of loam and peaty mold
Rich earth to feed the roots of growing stuff,
>   Stout trunks with branches sinewy and tough,
And tender leaves veined like a baby's hand
>   Drawing their strength and beauty from the land.

I love flat land where quiet orchards grow,
>   And little winds sing softly as they blow,
Across the fields where sheep and cattle graze,
>   Cooling the heat of sultry summer days,
As the long summer twilight settles down,
>   Upon the little houses of the town.

I love flat roads that seem to stretch away,
>   Beyond the narrow borders of today,
Into some never-never land where we
>   May find tall castles by a shining sea,
But for today I'll take a quiet field,
>   With a bright sun above it like a shield.

from "GOLDEN ROAD"

VILLAGE LADIES' AID

The room is filled with warmth and gaiety,
    As forty women crowd each other out,
Talking and laughing like a bunch of kids;
    Many of them a little plump and stout,
With strands of silver showing in their hair,
    And nice dark dresses that such women wear.

They start the meeting with a word of prayer,
    An old hymn sung with piety and grace
A verse or two of Scripture sweetly read,
    That seems to fit into the little place,
Because it tells of home and people who,
    Did just about the same things that we do.

From the bright kitchen comes the fragrant whiff
    Of coffee being made . . . the homey smell
Of sandwiches and cake and buttered scones,
    A sweet delicious warmth no words can tell,
Of fellowship and love and kindly thought,
    Within the walls of a small kitchen caught.

I sometimes think that in this atmosphere
    Of friendliness we touch the shining hem
Of the great inner meaning of the word
    To 'love thy neighbor' and in serving them
The commonplace is touched by the divine,
    And cake and tea become His bread and wine.

For in a little village once were laid,
The strong foundations of our ladies' aid.

from "HILLS OF HOME"

18

MY DAD . . . THE SAILOR

*(My father was the captain of a ship sailing the
Great Lakes, but he left that and went west and got a
homestead in 1902)*

He taught us all the weather signs,
　　A ring around the moon,
The scud of clouds above the mast,
　　The crying of a loon.

He told of things beyond our ken,
　　Queer laughter in the night,
The ghostly hulls of ships that rode,
　　Beyond the yardarm's light.

He spoke of harbor lights that shone,
　　Out of the mist and foam,
The glow of sunrise in the east,
　　The welcome lights of home.

He spoke of lonely graves that lie
　　Deep on the oceans' floors,
Of signs and wonders that he saw,
　　On lonely far-off shores.

And though he lived his length of days,
The sea was in his heart . . . always.

A HAPPY WOMAN

I met a happy woman
    Whose face was calm and sweet,
Who loved her home and all therein,
    The folks along her street;
She praised her children, told how nice
    They were to her and Dad,
And seemed to take a special joy
    In everything she had.

The morning glories climbing up
    Around her kitchen door,
She seemed to think she'd never grown
    Such lovely ones before,
Shop windows filled with glowing fruit —
    Spring flowers on display,
Set every fibre of her heart,
    To dancing for the day.

She didn't need a coach and four,
    To make her day complete,
She made her round of friendly calls,
    On her own sturdy feet,
Enjoying everyone she met
    And leaving in her wake,
A trail of happiness that spread,
    Like ripples on a lake.

I think the secret of her charm,
    Was just in being wise
Enough to see the simple things
    With clear contented eyes;
Holding aloft the precious flag
    Of piety and grace
A happy woman growing old,
    With laughter on her face.

from "HILLS OF HOME"

BURNING THE CHURCH MORTGAGE

We burned the mortgage of the church,
    In thankfulness and pride,
The minister and other folk
    All standing side by side,
The elders . . . ushers . . . ladies' aid,
    In one great moment met,
All proud as Lucifer to think
    Their church was free of debt.

The candles on the table shine,
    Like beacons from afar,
Reflecting somehow in their glow,
    The color of a star,
The pungent smell of melting wax,
    Hangs in the quiet air,
And faces in their tender light
    Are lovely as a prayer.

What countless hours of weary toil,
    What sales of cakes and pies,
How many dinners in the church,
    It took to realize,
The dollars to redeem the bond,
    But now the debt is paid,
Thanks to the faithful men who worked,
    Thanks to the ladies' aid.

from "FIRESIDE POEMS"

FRIENDSHIP

You have to work at friendship
    Like a gardener with his flowers,
Cherish the tiny buds of love,
    Treasure the happy hours,
Plant loving seeds for future bloom
    Pluck out the weeds and tares,
Water the soil with loving deeds,
    And firm it down with prayers.

You have to work at friendship,
    With tenderness and zeal,
Drawing your friends into your heart,
    With roots as strong as steel,
Shaping the growth with loving thought
    As careful gardeners do,
If love and peace and happiness
    Will ever bloom for you.

For friendship is a tender plant,
    Of bud and root and vine,
Frail as the mist above the hills,
    Fragrant as myrrh and pine,
Rooted in earth its branches reach
    Beyond the farthest sea,
Yet clings in little tender words,
    Between my friend and me.

And like all worthwhile things, it pays
Dividends in a hundred ways.

from "HILLS OF HOME"

OLD USHER

He squeaks around the little quiet aisles,
   Piling the hymn books up in tidy stacks,
Dusts off a chair . . . sorts the communion cards,
   Straightens some pamphlets on the little racks.

He holds a session with the janitor,
   Mentions a broken pane of glass upstairs,
Looks in the coal bin, shakes his head a bit,
   Straightens a row of kindergarten chairs.

That faint peculiar odor of a church
   Lies like old incense on the quiet air,
The scent of wood and wax and polished pews,
   And all the people who have worshipped there.

He stands a moment with a reverent look
   At the great window with its blues and gold,
Where Christ — the Shepherd — gathers up his lambs,
   And leads them to the shelter of a fold.

He shows the people to their waiting pews,
   Welcomes a stranger with a nod and smile,
Helps an old man take off his overcoat,
   Pilots a timid lady down the aisle.

He serves the preacher with a kindly grace,
   Lending a hand in scores of thoughtful ways,
And in his loving service to mankind,
   He finds a happiness beyond all praise.

from "HILLS OF HOME"

O WESTERN WIND

O western wind blow softly here,
    Bring me the scent of sage and brier
Wild mint around a brimming slough
    And blue smoke from a prairie fire,
Drifting like pale ghosts in the sky,
    Where clouds of tufted wool go by.

O western wind — blow gently here,
    Bring to my heart the thrilling sight
Of April skies serene and blue —
    Wild mallards in their northern flight,
Cleaving the sky in a long V
    Calling to something deep in me.

O western wind — I hear you blow,
    Above the rooftops of the East,
Inviting me to come once more
    To share in some great pagan feast,
Where wind and sun and everything,
    Drink to the coming of the Spring.

O western wind — that calls us home,
    We who are prairie born and bred,
With music from a magic flute,
    By some enchanted piper led,
Down prairie trails to the world's rim
    Where hearts beat high to follow him.

from "HILLS OF HOME"

WINTER MORNING

A morning crisp as watered silk,
    With blankets of new fallen snow,
Tucking the little houses in,
    For fear their naked feet will show,
The trees and shrubs are beautiful,
    Wrapped in their coats of carded wool.

The children on their way to school
    In knitted caps and scarlet coats,
Play hide and seek behind the drifts,
    Their laughter rises high and floats,
Above the highest maple trees
    Like half forgotten melodies.

The shop where mother buys her bread
    Has glittering panes of frosted glass,
Through which the lights take on a glow,
    Like holy candles at a mass,
The streets are paved with softest down,
    As if a king had come to town.

A sleigh goes by with chiming bells,
    Young people riding for a lark,
Their merry voices seem to ring,
    With extra sweetness in the dark,
As if they tasted suddenly
    How lovely simple things can be.

When Earth puts on her ermine wrap
And holds white diamonds in her lap.

from "GOLDEN ROAD"

COUNTRY CHURCH

It's little and shabby and dear knows when
    Its walls were done or the carpet new
But you sort of forget these little things
    As you sit in a wide old-fashioned pew,
Letting the peace of the autumn day
    Steal your worry and fear away.

And you think of the people who came and went
    Through the wide old door with its iron latch,
The plain good people of yesteryear
    Who sleep outside in the sunny patch
Of a little churchyard green and small
    Where the leaves of autumn so softly fall.

And the very walls seem to hold somehow
    The hymns they sang and the prayers they said,
The christening hymns for the little folk
    The comforting ones for the quiet dead,
The Christmas carols, the hymns of praise
    The harvest songs for Thanksgiving days.

The little rooms of the Sunday school
    Have tiny tables and painted chairs,
Where the children learn from the ancient books
    The meaning of worship and faith and prayers,
Setting a pattern of peace and joy
    Into the heart of a girl or boy.

No wonder the church at the crossroad gleams
With the honest earth and the stuff of dreams.

from "GOLDEN ROAD"

FARM ANIMALS

A collie dog with faithful eyes
    Who lives on trust and never tries
To reason out the right or wrong,
    He seems somehow to just belong
To an old farmyard . . . summer days,
    And the calm peace of country ways.

A Holstein cow's serene old face
    Seems to fit in a country place,
(Like clover fields and honey bees)
    Lying beneath a clump of trees,
Or grazing on a hilltop high
    A silhouette against the sky.

An old horse at the furrow's end,
    Is true and steady as a friend,
Part of the very land he plows,
    Of quiet fields and fragrant mows,
He asks so little for his pay
    A quiet stall . . . a fork of hay.

What of old hens who scold and talk
    And scratch their way around the walk?
Looking for handouts from the door.
    A kitten sleeping on the floor,
In a warm patch of noonday sun
    At perfect peace with everyone.

How lone and barren life would be
Without their gentle company.

from "GOLDEN ROAD"

SOUNDS OF PEACE

I love the sounds of peace about my ears,
    The slow and steady ticking of a clock,
A quiet river running to the sea,
    The homey chatter of a farmyard flock.

The whirr of quiet wings above the roof,
    An old cow slowly chewing on her cud,
A flock of sheep beneath a maple tree,
    An apple falling with a little thud.

I love the sound of people in a church,
    The choir coming in in cap and gown,
The old bell ringing in its ivied tower,
    Sending its echoes half across the town.

The sound of oars somewhere beyond the mist
    As early fishermen put out to sea,
The creak of branches in the dead of night,
    As a small wind goes by and rocks a tree.

The crackle of a fire in the grate,
    A kettle on the stove that softly sings,
I am so glad that I have ears to hear
    The little muted sounds of quiet things.

from "GOLDEN ROAD"

LAKE ONTARIO

I love the lake in all its many moods,
    Slate grey in wintertime, and in the spring
A soft Italian blue that seems to melt
    Into the sky — where clouds are on the wing,
Like birds who have a special rendezvous
    Somewhere beyond these miles of shining blue.

I love to see the freighters going by
    Weaving a pattern intricate as lace,
Sending up plumes of smoke into the sky,
    Like a tall flower rising from a vase,
That falls again to follow in its wake,
    Leaving a smudge of blue upon the lake.

Sailboats that skim across the placid blue,
    Like white birds flying low before a storm,
A fishing boat rocks gently to itself,
    Like an old lady delicate and warm,
Basking in sunlight in a garden chair,
    Folding her thin old hands to say a prayer.

And so the lake is part of all we are,
    The villages above a rocky ledge,
Great cities draw their lifeblood from her breast,
    The fertile farms that skirt the water's edge,
The camp site lovely as an artist's dream,
    A lighthouse sending out a golden beam.

Turquoise or cobalt blue or leaden grey,
I love this lake of ours just any way.

from "GOLDEN ROAD"

REMEMBRANCES

A pressed rose from a bride's bouquet,
    That someone loved and tucked away,
Between the pages of a book;
    A blurred old snap that someone took
That caught as in a fleeting glance
    One precious moment of romance.

A stoppered bottle of perfume
    Given a bridesmaid by a groom
Who has been dead these forty years;
    A hankie never meant for tears,
A square of Irish lace and lawn,
    With tiny stitched initials on.

An old book of the British Isles,
    A lady's magazine with styles
Of half a century ago;
    A Christmas card of drifted snow,
Showing a church with open doors,
    From which the golden lamplight pours.

A horsehair wreath . . . a tiny shoe
    I wonder if the mother knew
How far the little feet would stray,
    And die ten thousand miles away
Where blood-red sand and desert skies
    Keep watch above him where he lies.

A keepsake precious as a gem
Reminding her of each of them.

from "GOLDEN ROAD"

31

BUILDING A NATION

It isn't battlefields and guns
    That make a nation great,
Or clanking arms or marching men
    Or panoply of State,
It isn't pageantry or power
    Where Might and Triumph ride,
For kingdoms are not built on war
    Or nations fed on pride.

It's little homes against the earth
    Where peace and love abide,
It's rugged hills and quiet fields,
    Across the countryside,
It's children trudging off to school
    Secure and clean and gay,
Who own the right to childhood land
    The right to laugh and play.

It's stony fields and little brooks,
    With hidden age-old springs,
It's tender songs of youth and love
    That some old mother sings,
It's love of home and firelight,
    It's sweat and faith and toil,
The souls of men who earn their bread,
    From sun and rain and soil.

It's churches built on quiet streets,
    It's winding roads and downs,
It's apple orchards in the sun
    And prosperous cheerful towns,
It's cattle on a hundred hills,
    In pastures green and sweet,
And happiness that sets a seal
    On faces that you meet.

It's something deeper still than this,
    Beyond our thought and ken,
The faith that sees the good that lives
    Within the hearts of men,
A woman glad to bear a child
    Protected by her mate,
It's home and love . . . and little fields,
    That make a nation great.

from "KITCHEN WINDOW"

THE HIGHWAY

There is a song that the tires sing
    As they roll along with a dip and swing,
Over the hills and down the dales
    Like a stout old ship with flowing sails,
A song as old as the heart of man,
    Born in the wheels of a caravan.

It sings of wonders beyond the rim
    Of the next wide hill . . . of shadows dim
That hover behind the line of trees,
    That only the eyes of a lover see,
A lover of distance and open space,
    With a sweet wind blowing against your face.

It tells of love like a beacon light,
    Beyond the rim of a prairie night,
Of mountains rising to snow clad peaks,
    And the glacier mother of mountain creeks,
Rushing along to the far-off sea,
    Deep as the walls of eternity.

The glimpse of a home as you hurry by
    A white wash glowing against the sky,
A little yard where a small boy plays;
    Of winter evenings and summer days,
Packed with the drama of common stuff,
    Into a pattern rich and rough.

Life and death and a hundred things
And held in the song that a tire sings.

from "GOLDEN ROAD"

34

GOLDEN THINGS

I love the sheen of golden things
    The light that catches wedding rings
A bright gold watch on a good chain,
    A dandelion washed by rain.

A blue white diamond set in gold,
    June butter in a wooden mold,
Apricot jam . . . an ear of corn,
    A soldier's medal proudly worn.

A field of golden ripened wheat
    Basking in waves of harvest heat,
When earth and sky and air are one,
    Holding the radiance of the sun.

The first bright tulips in the spring,
    The flash of sunlight on a wing,
The shimmer of a jewelled clip,
    The golden prow of an old ship.

Tight golden curls that frame the face
    Of a small boy . . . the golden lace,
In the white bodice of a bride;
    Tall candles by an altar side.

The golden embers of a fire,
    Light striking on a tall church spire,
Sunset and sunrise . . . jasper walls,
    Upon whose face the sunlight falls.

There are so many golden things,
That beggars are as rich as kings.

from "GOLDEN ROAD"

UNIVERSAL THINGS

There are so many universal things
    That all men love — I think I'll make a list —
First will be homes and firelight within,
    A field of clover that the sun has kissed,
Unruffled water in a still lagoon
    The splendor of an autumn afternoon.

A young lamb nuzzling at the mother's flanks,
    An old chick hen covering her tiny flock,
With her wide wings, settling them for the night;
    The slow and steady ticking of a clock
As if the very pulse of Time itself,
    Was speaking from a cretonne-covered shelf.

There are so many universal things
    That we can find to make us all akin,
A pot of homemade soup upon the stove,
    A little cookie jar of painted tin,
Sorrow and hardship . . . poverty and care,
    The blessed comfort of a word of prayer.

A new born baby in a woolen shawl,
    An old man doing up his nightly chores,
A fisherman in an old battered boat,
    Counting his fish or resting on his oars,
While there across the water clear and green,
    The lights of little houses can be seen.

And in them all — like a rare perfume clings,
The brotherhood of universal things.

from "FIRESIDE POEMS"

THE MARITIMER

His heart is in the Maritimes
 Where spicy salt winds blow,
He hears the wind come up the Gulf,
 Laden with frost and snow,
Where green waves breaking on a beach,
 Fills him with joy too deep for speech.

There is a flavor to the air
 Drawn from the salt and brine,
That inland people never know,
 Sweet as old country wine,
But Maritimers know the taste
 Of the Atlantic's stormy waste.

The wild sweet breath of headland grass,
 Of sun drenched miles of beach,
And driftwood newly sawn and piled;
 A sea gull's lonely screech,
The sight of icebergs riding high,
 Like broken castles in the sky.

His heart is in the Maritimes,
 Where an old village stands,
Half hidden by tall trees and vines,
 Scoured by drifted sands,
Where the bleached ribs of codfish racks,
 Hobnob with lonely fisher shacks.

All this he sees on lonely nights,
When he can't sleep for city lights.

from "FIRESIDE POEMS"

ROSEBUSH

She holds a little shrub with tender care
    Dead looking, lifeless, packed in peat and moss,
She bought it at the five and ten today,
    The people notice her and smile across
The crowded car . . . at her old shopping bag,
    And little rosebush with its wooden tag.

They smile and nod because they understand
    Just how she feels . . . and why it means so much
To carry home a little rooted tree,
    And why her fingers have a loving touch,
Holding the brittle bush with special care,
    Lest someone crush the tiny branches there.

She'll plant it where the morning sunlight falls,
    And watch the small green leaves uncurl and spread,
Their little eager fingers to the light;
    Add mulch and fertilizer to the bed,
Set up a lattice . . . train the tiny shoots,
    Keep the soil clean and moist around the roots.

And when it blooms, no rose in all the world
    Will be as lovely as her tiny one,
No fragrance half so sweet, no leaves so green,
    And when it sways half opened in the sun
Something of her . . . the deep eternal part
    Will shed its beauty from the rose's heart.

from "FIRESIDE POEMS"

FAMILIAR THINGS

I love familiar things . . . an old clock's face
    A kitchen shelf with a bright cretonne frill,
An old chair with a patchwork cushion on,
    Petunias on a painted window sill.

An old grey barn whose weather-beaten ends
    Have known the lashing tides of wind and rain,
A cup and saucer from an ancient set
    Of sturdy chinaware severely plain.

Buck brush and willow scrub . . . a rutted trail
    Worn deep and smooth by quiet homing hoofs,
A narrow gabled window in a house,
    Soft mossy ridges on old shingled roofs.

I love a kindly face with patient eyes
    Where wrinkles etch a story brave and fine,
Whose understanding heart and quiet strength,
    Is written like a scroll in every line.

A homemade quilt . . . a small wood-burning stove,
    A little rocker that your mother had,
A little cape hung up behind the door,
    An overcoat that once belonged to Dad.

Old shabby bits, I know, yet in each thing
Something of them seems to forever cling.

from "FIRESIDE POEMS"

IRELAND

I have a smidgen of Irish in me
    And so when the night comes 'round,
I'll be thinkin' of peat fires smolderin' like
    And shamrocks that cover the ground.

I'll be back where the fairies are playin' their tricks,
    Like kids by the edge of the bog,
As the old folks come wandering hand in hand
    Like ghosts comin' out of the fog.

There'll be Donohues . . . Caseys . . . O'Connors galore
    And the family o' Michael O'Shane,
And the wicked old widow who walks with a limp
    And lives at the turn of the lane.

Clancy will give us a song on the pipes
    Weird as the cry of a loon,
'Twill echo from here to the brow o' the hill,
    Sweet as an old-fashioned tune.

Oh it's Irish I am with a bit of a brogue,
    And warm is me heart to me own,
If it's Irish indeed to the end of the earth,
    Sure you'll never be walkin' alone.

CHERRIES AND ROBINS

Cherries and robins go hand in hand,
    Bread and butter and sun and sand.
A nest high up in an apple tree,
    A white sail showing upon the sea.

A little boy in a clean blue suit,
    A shepherd playing a silver flute,
A church on a hill with a golden spire,
    An old man dozing before the fire.

Two by two as the years go by,
    We see the wonder of sea and sky,
A hill that touches the prairie's rim,
    A purple valley remote and dim.

A mother . . . a child and a house somewhere,
    A lullaby and a word of prayer,
These are the things in the life of Man,
    That have never changed since the world began.

Cherries and robins and bittersweet,
And little houses along the street.

I LOVE A LITTLE GROWING THING

I love a little growing thing,
    That sticks its nose up in the spring,
Above a cold and frozen ground,
    When there is nothing much around.

A tiny bush brave as a knight,
    Whose little leaves are rolled up tight,
Who dares to tell them to unfold,
    In spite of icy winds and cold.

A crocus dressed in fuzzy fur,
    Feels the small life within it stir,
And lo a flower pokes its head,
    Above a frozen flower bed.

A bush that wintered by the well,
    Has such a fairy tale to tell,
Of dreams within its shiny bark,
    Of voices whispering in the dark.

For Life can hold such shining hours,
    New budded trees and scarlet flowers,
The blessed faith in life that springs,
    From the deep heart of growing things.

BE CAREFUL, MOTHER

"Be careful, mother" — what a lovely phrase
    As now the weak is guided by the strong,
Taking small steps to match the slower stride,
    The daughter sort of inches her along,
Toward a car parked in an uptown lot,
    Guiding her gently to the sheltered spot.

"Be careful, mother" — how the sentence glows
    Amid the careless babble everywhere,
The sidewalk turmoil and the weary feet,
    These gentle words like music on the air,
Reminding us that somewhere Love is lord,
    And there are old folks sheltered and adored.

"Be careful, mother" — as they move along
    The faltering footsteps and the valiant young,
It seems the very air is filled with sound,
    And high above the street a bell is rung,
Proclaiming to the world a great event,
    Or some good tidings that a king had sent;

Because a daughter, beautiful and strong
Guided a pair of trembling feet along.

from "Backdoor Neighbors"

43

THE WORDS OF JESUS

The words of Jesus were such simple things,
    He never clothed His thought in cult and creeds,
Just spoke of homes and bread and fireshine,
    The little common run of human needs,
A woman weaving linen, carding wool,
    A farmer's measuring basket flowing full.

He found a precious unity of love
    Between a mother hen and God's great care,
He loved small ships and little fishing smacks,
    Made friends of all the people working there,
A fisher mending nets . . . a child who brought
    A little basket for the fish he'd caught.

He knew the farmers and their tiny fields,
    The shepherds and their flocks, the quiet fold,
The lost one on the mountain far away,
    All these were in the stories that He told,
The parables that spoke of simple things,
    People they knew from shepherd boys to kings.

He clothed religion in a homespun cloak
    And wrapped the Father's love in common dress,
So all might know its true simplicity,
    He gave the meanest flower a loveliness,
And made the door of heaven wide and broad,
    That all might see the fatherhood of God.

from "BACKDOOR NEIGHBORS"

MY DAUGHTER

She tells me that my hair's a mess
She jerks and twitches at my dress
And riles me often I confess,
      My daughter.

She moons around the house and sings,
And shudders at old-fashioned things,
She's modern as a Spitfire's wings,
      My daughter.

She's restless, moody, filled with fears,
Changes from laughter into tears,
Apes every movie star she hears,
      My daughter.

She's going to wed a millionaire
(She says) and have fine clothes to wear,
Peaches and cream her daily fare,
      My daughter.

She combs her hair in dainty swirls,
Sets bobby pins to hold the curls,
And imitates the other girls,
      My daughter.

Although she's all these things I tell
And many more . . . she's doing well,
And I — her mother — think she's swell,
      My daughter.

from "AUNT HATTIE'S PLACE"

I LOVE BRIGHT THINGS

I love bright things — a blue cup for my tea,
 A pottery plate bright as an orange skin,
A drinking glass with yellow tulips on,
 The gaudy sparkle of a jewelled pin.

I love a tablecloth where roses bloom
 Cheerful and gay as any flower bed,
Red hollyhocks beside a garden wall,
 A pewter plate to hold my daily bread.

I love bright curtains draped in tiny folds,
 To let the gleaming bars of sunlight through,
A cushion on a chair of colored blocks,
 A tiny woven rug of turquoise blue.

I love a crimson coat gay as a flag,
 A white sail poised above a quiet sea,
The royal blue of grapes . . . the sheen of silk,
 Red candles shining on a Christmas tree.

I love blue lightning . . . raindrops on a wire,
 A golden hilltop . . . planes with silver wings,
The world is beautiful and fair to me,
 I have the company of lovely things.

from "AUNT HATTIE'S PLACE"

THE OLD MOTHER

(To my Mother)

She is so new to Heaven . . . let her be
    Quiet a while — she always said to me
She'd like to rest a long, long time, and then
    She wouldn't mind taking up Life again,
If they would let her have a little yard
    To sort of putter in, she tried so hard
To make things grow — and always loved the clean
    Sweet breath of flowers and the leaves' new green,
When April washed the sky and May came down
    Like a young bride arrayed in cap and gown.

And oh, dear Father, let her have a chair
    To rock upon a wide veranda there,
She worked so hard and, oh, her calloused feet
    Would find tough going on a golden street,
Farm women have so little time for pleasure
    Steady back-breaking toil the mete and measure
Of their days — and so for Heaven's adorning
    Let her grow young and lovely as the morning,
Forgetting in the peace of Heaven's ways
    The old heart-breaking toil of prairie days.

from "AUNT HATTIE'S PLACE"

HOMEBODIES

(To my Grandmother)

Content with little sunny rooms,
    With kitchen clean and bright,
A rocking chair beside the hearth,
    And shelter in the night;
The shiny stove and Dad's old chair,
    A mat beside the door,
Gay flowers on the window sill,
    A clean old painted floor.

She wears a starched red cotton dress,
    An apron trimmed with lace,
Soft hair that makes a sort of frame
    Around her quiet face,
She has a few old trusted friends,
    Her love is safe and near,
A steady, gracious soul that shines,
    From eyes serene and clear.

She makes such fragrant homemade bread,
    Such pickles and such jam,
She's always cooking something nice,
    A spicy home cured ham,
Her garden is a friendly place
    Of sweet old-fashioned bloom,
Where mignonette and marigold,
    Are heavy with perfume.

Could Life hold more than little homes,
  Secure from greed and spoil,
The quiet beauty of the stars,
  The fragrance of the soil,
A heart at peace with all the world,
  Content with simple things,
She holds within her quiet rooms,
  The best that Heaven brings.

from "KITCHEN WINDOW"

I CARRIED HIS CROSS

*(There is an old tradition that a black man carried
the cross and in this poem he is the speaker)*

I carried His cross on that fearful day,
    As He stumbled along on the narrow way,
The stones were cruel on His bleeding feet,
    As we walked along on that cobbled street.

The soldiers pushed at the watching throng,
    Clearing the way as we moved along,
Their bright swords gleamed in the morning light,
    As we bowed in the face of the Roman might.

The way was long and the dawn was chill,
    As we toiled along to that lonely hill,
And some of them jeered and some of them cried,
    As I carried the cross of the crucified.

The crosses were set and the black deed done,
    As darkness descended to hide the sun,
The veil of the Temple was rent in twain
    As He hung all day in cruel pain.

On that lonely hilltop of Calvary,
Some of them there . . . were black like me.

I HEAR FROM HER AT CHRISTMAS

I hear from her at Christmas,
    And oh I am so glad,
To once again renew the warmth
    Of friendship that we had,
Although she lives so far away,
    We are still friends on Christmas Day.

She writes about her children,
    And the way they're getting on,
What they are doing . . . how they fare,
    And all but one is gone,
The house seems empty-like and bare,
    Without their happy presence there.

She says that Dad is slowing up,
    His hair is white as snow,
And sometimes I feel weary-like,
    (We all get old you know)
But Christmas with its happy cheer,
    Brings the old friends forever near.

And though she lives so far away,
We are old friends on Christmas Day.

51

CLEAN THINGS

I like to lie in a still darkened room
    And think of all the clean things that I know,
Sand filtered water in a country well,
    The white unearthly purity of snow.

A new plowed field of steaming virgin sod,
    A white beach when the tide is going out,
The crumpled newness of unfolding leaves,
    A small pig with his tiny wrinkled snout.

New coppers shining as the purest gold,
    A scoured step . . . the clean scales of a fish,
The white deck of a ship . . . a gleaming sail,
    The pearly lustre of a china dish.

The smell of mint and apple trees in bloom
    A field of lupins . . . new hay in a mow,
The brass tipped horns of oxen in the sun
    New sheaves . . . the shiny moldboard of a plow.

The sheen of pewter . . . old plates on a rail,
    Small whitewashed stones in little tidy rings,
The world is never lonely to me now,
    I have the company of lovely things.

from "BESIDE STILL WATERS"

SPRING'S HERALD

A frog is such a weesome thing
    To be a herald of the spring,
From the old slough behind the trees
    They always sing on nights like these,
Their cheerful tuneless melody,
    That seems a part of spring to me.

And I remember dusk and dawn,
    Bringing to me Saskatchewan,
Night like a blanket thick and cool
    Stars white as lilies in a pool,
The wind's cry in the hollow mow,
    Gulls flying low behind the plow.

In fancy I can hear the birds
    Telling their love in tender words,
And through the haze of April heat,
    The tiny fingers of the wheat,
Lift up the soil so eagerly,
    From their small caskets to be free.

Far from its peace, my heart still clings
    To the warm joy of bygone springs,
The wide brown fields where cloud and sun
    Make the long dappled shadows run;
The glowing furnaces of dawn,
    Bringing to me . . . Saskatchewan.

from "BESIDE STILL WATERS"

IN AN OLD TRUNK

A little crochet bonnet for a doll
    A bit of tatting that my sister made,
A fragile cup and saucer in a box,
    A parting present from the ladies' aid,
A few old tintypes almost faded out,
    A snap of Maw before she got so stout.

This in the till — and in the bottom part,
    A piece of fur wrapped up away from moths,
A few old-fashioned hairpins and a comb,
    A yellow set of kitchen tablecloths,
Two baby dresses and a tiny boot,
    Some braid ripped off an old beloved suit.

Such worthless things, you say — I know they are —
    And yet I hold them dear because they mean
So many things . . . days that will ne'er return,
    They keep the flowers of memory ever green,
A little shrine in an old attic high
    Where I can go on rainy days . . . to cry.

from "BESIDE STILL WATERS"

THE OLD PREACHER

He was a little man with greying hair,
    That hung in straggly wisps around his neck,
Curling a bit as if he were a child,
    He wore a shabby suit of brownish check,
His coat bagged in around the knees a bit,
    With many wrinkles where he used to sit.

He'd mount the pulpit like a ragged knight,
    Smooth back his hair and straighten up his coat,
Hunt for his text, and cough behind his hand,
    Peer through his spectacles and clear his throat,
And read a Psalm in an old voice that shook,
    Turning the thin worn pages of The Book.

And yet when Death was close his gentle face
    Shone like a light when darkness gathered near,
His steady hand upon a fevered brow,
    His quiet voice would banish pain and fear,
And many walking in the shadows dim,
    Went comforted and glad because of him.

I sometimes think God has a special grace
    For little unassuming folk like these,
Surely we need their kindly ministry,
    The humble way they work to try to please,
No earthly trumpets sound their loud acclaim,
    And yet they conquer kingdoms in His name.

from "BESIDE STILL WATERS"

IN HEAVEN

(A prayer)

Please let there be a few familiar things,
    A quiet orchard where a robin sings,
A clump of trees outlined against a hill,
    A little brook whose song is never still.

Let there be kids on little three-wheeled bikes,
    I always love to see the little tikes,
Wheeling and puffing as they ride along;
    The homesick longing in a cowboy's song.

I hope that I may have an apple tree,
    To grow beside a hill and comfort me,
And books upon a sturdy hanging shelf,
    Where you can browse around and help yourself.

Let there be rocking chairs and little stools,
    To rest your feet upon . . . and shiny pools,
Where water lilies bloom and fishes hide,
    Along the tangled rushes at the side.

And if You do not mind . . . a glowing hearth,
A friend or two that I had known on Earth.

TODAY

I am going to enjoy myself today,
    No matter what comes, I am going to say
"Well isn't that nice, who would ever have thought
    Of the lovely things that the day has brought."

I'll smile at people I do not know,
    And wish them well . . . as I watch them go
Along the street or a shopping mall,
    Buying fruit from a country stall.

I will speak to a child in a shiny pram,
    Holding a tiny wooly lamb,
Smile at his mother and share her joy,
    Admire the curls of her little boy.

I will sing . . . perhaps in a squeaky key,
    And the young folks will snicker and smile at me,
But I will not mind . . . for I know that they
    Will come to the turn of the road some day.

And I hope they are happy and well content,
Glad in the thought of a life well spent.

THE PART O' ME THAT'S IRISH

Oh the part o' me that's Irish
 Wint to sleep the other night,
I heard the leprechauns a-whine
 Across the lonely night,
And mingled in the bog land breeze,
 I smelt the bitter smoke,
Of turf fires smolderin' in the dark,
 The laugh o' fairy folk.

I saw the piper-man go by
 Paradin' wi' his tunes;
The old soft mist above the bog,
 The laughter o' the loons,
I saw the white o' sheeted dead,
 Above the clamorin' sea,
And felt the tuggin' o' the tide
 Against the heart o' me.

And I wint by a cottage door,
 And by a castle stair,
Rememberin' through the blood o' me,
 The ghosts o' people there,
And felt against the quiverin' sky,
 The singin' o' the lark,
And heard the wee folk o' the bog,
 All dancin' in the dark.

And in my dreams a peat fire glowed,
    And we were gathered round,
All the old folks of other days
    That's buried in the ground,
But up from all the graves they came,
    A-trailin' mist and shine,
These gay old people o' the race
    Whose blood and bone is mine.

So the part o' me that's Irish,
    Claimed kinship wi' the dead,
And listened to their merry laugh
    And all the things they said,
We saw again the lashin' seas,
    The green o' fairy rings,
And driftin' down across the bogs,
    The smell of Irish springs.

from "BESIDE STILL WATERS"

FARM HOMES

I like a kitchen big enough
    To hold a rocking chair,
With windows looking to the sun,
    And flowers blooming there,
I like big cupboards by the wall,
    That hold a lot of things,
The cups hung up on little hooks;
    A yellow bird that sings.

I like to do my mending there,
    Where I can watch the road,
And see the teams come plodding home,
    And smell their fragrant load,
Of heavy sheaves at stacking time,
    Or hear the wagons creak,
And groan beneath their golden weight,
    If it is threshing week.

I like to have the supper on,
    And let it simmer slow,
With rich brown gravy bubbling up,
    Around the meat, you know,
With apple pie set out to cool
    And flaky new baked bread,
With golden syrup in a bowl,
    And jelly warm and red.

I like to have the lamps a-shine,
　　With yellow glowing light,
And have the kitchen warm and clean,
　　When they come in at night,
To make a home so snug and dear,
　　That when they work or play,
They hold a picture in their hearts,
　　Of home at close of day.

from "BESIDE STILL WATERS"

ONTARIO COUNTRYSIDE

Oh I have loved the beauty of the world,
    The brooks half hidden in their ferny banks,
Sorrel and blue eyed vetch and bittersweet . . .
    And in the early spring the golden ranks
Of daffodils that march across the lawn,
    Like warriors with their battle plumage on.

I have loved elm and birch and knotty pine,
    Red maple, cedar . . . clumps of evergreen,
A thrush at dawn . . . a little air-borne seed
    Old woodland pools where weeping willows lean,
A path half hidden in the dappled shade,
    Patterned like figures in an old brocade.

I have loved cups and thin transparent bowls,
    And delft blue teapots . . . little wicker chairs,
Old houses made of stone . . . wide gracious halls,
    The rounded symmetry of curving stairs,
Wide dressing tables . . . flacons of perfume,
    A golden fire flickering in a room.

I have loved people, country-wise and good,
    Who tread the simple quiet ways of earth,
Acquainted with the sunrise and the night,
    Aware of death . . . of tragedy and birth,
People whose hearts are somehow closely knit,
    With God's good world and all the joy of it.

from "ROSES IN DECEMBER"

MY KITCHEN WINDOW

My kitchen window is above the sink,
    With dotted curtains looped in tiny folds,
A frame for mountains and a bit of sea;
    And all day long it glows and shines and holds,
A hundred pictures for my heart's delight,
    People who hurry by . . . and stars at night.

What matters if my work be drab and dull
    If I can lift my eyes from pots and pans,
And see a mountain etched against the sky,
    A fleet of clouds like shining caravans,
Setting their course for harbors dim and far,
    In some vast heaven where the blessed are.

I don't mind making pies and loaves of bread
    If I can look out from my window high
And see a little girl with flying hair,
    Poised on a scooter as she dashes by —
Such breathless sunny joy her heart must know,
    Seems leaven for a whole wide world of woe.

So my small window with its curtains prim
    Brings all the world a-knocking at my heart;
A mother passing by, a priest, a child,
    Makes me in tiny rooms a living part
Of all this glad good earth and makes me kin
    Of all the glory that has ever been.

from "KITCHEN WINDOW"

HEROES

(To an early missionary)

He should have worn a doublet and a sword,
    This little earnest worker of the Lord,
A suit of mail . . . a gleaming silver shield,
    To shed the arrows of Life's battlefield,
And yet his only armor was a creed,
    A loving sympathy for those in need.

He rode no prancing steed to meet the foe,
    (Rough were the lonely trails his feet would know),
No gallant ending of a high crusade,
    But little lonely shacks that men had made,
These were his temples, this his church and pew,
    A homesick woman and a child or two.

No foe to meet in ringing open fight,
    But lonely folk to comfort in the night,
No silver bugles sounding high and clear;
    He fought the unseen foes of hate and fear,
And battled bravely all his flags unfurled,
    Preaching his lowly gospel to the world.

No chancel rail to breathe his penance by
    (He holds communion with the earth and sky)
Spending his youth with glad and lavish hand
    To cheer and bless the people of his land;
He asks of earth no honor or reward,
    Only the grace to live . . . and serve his Lord.

from "WIDE HORIZONS"

HE NOTICED LITTLE THINGS

He noticed little things . . . the widow's mite
    A blind man trembling to receive his sight,
He used a small boy's lunch of fish and cake,
    To feed a multitude beside the lake.

He spoke of barley fields and threshing floors,
    The little daily round of household chores,
A woman making bread and using yeast,
    The happy bridegroom at the wedding feast.

He told of things beyond our human ken,
    The hidden power in the hearts of men,
A father's love . . . a mother's tender care,
    The beauty of the stars . . . a murmured prayer.

The lilies of the field . . . the ripened grain
    The cool and blessed healing of the rain,
These are the things He noticed on His way,
    Among the common people of His day.

In the bright reaches of Eternity
I wonder if he sometimes longs . . . for Galilee.

FEEL OF SPRING

There is a feel of springtime in the air,
    Although the distant hills are bleak and bare,
I heard a robin in a maple tree,
    Piping a tiny hymn of praise for me.

Beside the house in a warm sheltered spot,
    I found a cluster of forget-me-not,
Blue as the skies that circle overhead,
    And a small seedling in a flower bed.

My mother had brought down her garden shawl,
    She has a small niche near a sunny wall,
Where she can sit and watch the birds and sing,
    Her Irish songs . . . it's part of every spring.

Part of the earth and sky and crystal air,
    The essence of her faith and love and prayer,
The end of suffering and earthly strife,
    The glad renewing of eternal life.

For Spring renews our faith and lets us see,
The wide blue reaches of Eternity.

I KNOW ALL THIS

I know how warm and dim a barn can be
How soft a manger bed the Christ-child had,
Because when I was small I used to hold,
The lantern for my dad.

I know how sweet the breath of new mown hay,
How close the bonds with gentle beasts can be,
Because I tended cattle long ago,
And loved their ways with me.

I know the peace and quiet of the night,
How close the skies above a pasture are,
Because I walked where cowboys tend their herds,
And saw a star.

I know how mothers love the tender touch,
Of tiny fists and bodies soft and warm,
Because I held a child against my heart,
Safe from the storm.

I know all this — because I am a part
Of life's vast show — this street and church and store,
A scarlet sleigh . . . the chime of Christmas bells,
The wreath upon the door.

from "BACKDOOR NEIGHBORS"

I'M LIKE MY MOTHER

I'm like my mother — I can see
    Her every action here in me,
The very way she punched the bread,
    The things she wore and what she said,
The way she slanted up her eyes,
    Crimping the edges of the pies.

I catch myself unconsciously
    Doing the things I used to see
Her doing all around the place —
    The very crinkles in her face,
The lace-edged aprons that she wore,
    The way she bargained at the store.

I see myself in printed blue,
    Puttering just like she used to do,
Setting the table neat as wax,
    Putting out father's bedtime snacks,
Sitting down heavy in a chair,
    Panting a bit upon the stair.

And like my mother — I have known
    The toil and burdens . . . walked alone
Life's rugged road, the hopes and fears,
    That mother carried all the years,
Facing a world that takes its toll,
    Of all the strength of heart and soul.

I only pray, though years be long
I'll hold her laughter and her song.

from **"Backdoor Neighbors"**

BY BREAD ALONE

We do not live by bread alone — ah, no!
    We live by love and peace and fireglow,
By gentle thoughts and small deeds kindly done,
    By toil and weariness . . . laughter and fun,
By music's magic touch and love's dear hand,
    And childish feet that walk in wonderland.

We live by all the beauty of the world,
    Smoke from a supper fire softly curled,
Above the snowy rooftops of the town;
    By a tall lady in a satin gown,
With pearls twined in the meshes of her hair;
    We live by faith and solitude and prayer.

We live by toil the routine of a day,
    Small humble chores . . . dishes to put away,
A floor to scrub . . . an evening meal to cook,
    A little journey to return a book,
A gay excited girl to help along,
    Time out to listen to a robin's song.

We live by roses in a silver jar,
    By dawn and candlelight . . . by one blue star,
Shining above an airport where we wait,
    By love triumphant over war and hate,
A faithful king upon a steady throne,
    For no one ever lives by bread alone.

from "FIRESIDE POEMS"

I LOVE THE PEACE

I love the peace and quiet of the night,
   The glow of dawn . . . the sheen of candlelight,
The smell of wood smoke in the evening air,
   And someone singing in the dark somewhere.

I love the smell of apples in the fall,
   And blue grapes growing by a garden wall,
A stubble field where clumps of briers grow,
   The still and quiet coming of the snow.

I love the rutted paths that cattle make,
   Winding their way toward a nearby lake,
The way an old tree sheds its autumn leaves,
   The sound of water running in the eaves.

I love the sound of kids in happy play,
   In a small park toward the end of day,
A string of birds along a swinging wire,
   The smell of wood . . . the crackling of a fire.

All these dear homey things of every day,
God grant that naught can ever take away.

THINGS THEY'LL REMEMBER

When they are old — these are the sort of things
    They will remember as the years go by,
A little gilt-edged card with roses on,
    A fleece of carded clouds against the sky.

They will remember cookies warm and good,
    The taste of apples from a sun-warmed tree,
The feel of earth against their naked feet,
    The thrill of seeing ships put out to sea.

A dress she loved, a treasured pair of shoes,
    A doll that spoke . . . a little rocking chair,
A birthday cake with silver candles on,
    The fearful shadows falling on the stair.

A boy will treasure in his deepest heart,
    The memory of the dog who worshipped him,
The swimmin' hole . . . cool water on his feet,
    The shadows in a forest cool and dim.

They will remember — as the years go by
    Dreams lovely as the day . . . hope's shining wings,
Like incense for their soul's eternal peace
    The lovely comfort of remembered things.

from "BACKDOOR NEIGHBORS"

THIS CANADA

How could I bound it with one little page,
    Who holds such riches for her heritage,
How could I list with one rude stumbling pen
    A new world open to the eyes of men.
Or talk in little words of her at all
    Who holds me captive in her mighty thrall.

Her vast dominion sweeps from sea to sea,
    Yet little gardens hold the heart of me,
Small streets with houses set in tidy rows,
    Patches of ground where clumps of lilac grow,
And clean white clothes upon a line to dry,
    Making dear homely pictures on the sky.

How could I voice such dear eternal things
    As mating birds and hurrying eager wings,
Mothers who fold their thin old hands to pray,
    That last white star who waits to greet the day,
Hunger and thirst . . . supper and new baked bread,
    Sorrow so deep it can't be comforted.

And yet as long as this warm heart shall beat
    Her voice will sing of dawn above the wheat,
Of crumbling furrows laid in steaming rows,
    Dear homey fields where someone reaps and sows,
And kindly folk to love her budding flowers,
    This virgin land . . . this Canada of ours.

from "WIDE HORIZONS"

INDEX